W9-BMA-614

JIMMY SMITS

A Real-Life Reader Biography

Melanie Cole

Mitchell Lane Publishers, Inc.
P.O. Box 200 • Childs, Maryland 21916

HOUSTON PUBLIC LIBRARY

R01200 34228

DISCARD

Mitchell Lane
PUBLISHERS

Copyright © 1998 by Mitchell Lane Publishers. All rights reserved. No part of this book may be repro-
duced without written permission from the publisher. Printed and bound in the United States of
America.

Second Printing
Real-Life Reader Biographies

Selena	Robert Rodriguez	Mariah Carey	Rafael Palmeiro
Tommy Nuñez	Trent Dimas	Cristina Saralegui	Andres Galarraga
Oscar De La Hoya	Gloria Estefan	**Jimmy Smits**	Mary Joe Fernandez
Cesar Chavez	Celine Dion	Vanessa Williams	Sinbad
Shania Twain	Garth Brooks	Paula Abdul	Chuck Norris
Sammy Sosa	Mark McGwire	Brandy	Sheila E.
Mia Hamm	Michelle Kwan	Rosie O'Donnell	Jeff Gordon
Salma Hayek	Hollywood Hogan	Arnold Schwarzenegger	

Library of Congress Cataloging-in-Publication Data
Cole, Melanie, 1957–
    Jimmy Smits / Melanie Cole.
        p. cm. — (A real-life reader biography)
    Includes index.
    Summary: Presents a biography of the talented and versatile actor best known for his television
roles in "L.A. Law" and "NYPD Blue."
    ISBN 1-883845-59-9 (lib. bound)
    1. Smits, Jimmy—Juvenile literature. 2. Actors—United States—Biography—Juvenile literature.
3. Hispanic American actors—United States—Biography—Juvenile literature. [1. Smits, Jimmy. 2.
Actors and actresses. 3. Hispanic American actors. 4. Hispanic Americans—Biography.] I. Title. II.
Series.
PN2287. S614C66   1997
791.45'028'092—dc21   97-43445
[B]   CIP
                                                                                            AC

ABOUT THE AUTHOR: Melanie Cole has been a writer and editor for seventeen years. She was previously an associate editor of *Texas Monthly* and is now managing editor of *Hispanic* magazine. She has published numerous poems, articles, and reviews in various journals, magazines, and newspapers. She is also a contributing writer to the Mitchell Lane series **Famous People of Hispanic Heritage**. A native of Kansas, Ms. Cole now resides in Austin, Texas.

PHOTO CREDITS: cover: AP Photo/Rick Bowmer; p. 4 sketch by Barbara Tidman; p. 8 Twentieth Century Fox; p. 12 Globe Photos/Fitzroy Barrett; p. 17 Twentieth Century Fox; p. 18 Globe Photos; p. 21 Columbia Pictures; p. 22 Cinema Plus L.P.; p. 24 New Line Cinema/Rico Torres; p. 27 Globe Photos/ Fitzroy Barrett; p. 30 AP Photo

ACKNOWLEDGMENTS: The following story has been thoroughly researched and checked for accuracy. To the best of our knowledge, it represents a true story. Though we attempt to contact each person profiled in our Real-Life Reader Biographies, for various reasons, we were unable to authorize every story.

Table of Contents

Chapter 1
Finding a Place

When Jimmy Smits was a young boy, there were times when he felt like he didn't fit in. He spent much of his childhood on the tough streets of Brooklyn, New York. He also lived in Puerto Rico. Each time his family moved, Jimmy had to adjust to new friends and a new way of life.

Jimmy Smits was born in Brooklyn on July 9, 1955. Jimmy, his two younger sisters, and his parents lived in several neighborhoods in

Jimmy lived in Puerto Rico and Brooklyn when he was growing up.

Living in Puerto Rico was a shock because Jimmy did not speak Spanish.

New York City. His family moved back to Puerto Rico, his mother's home, when Jimmy was ten. His parents didn't want to move all the time, but they had to go where they could find jobs. They were hardworking people who had to make do with very little. Jimmy remembers walking around most of the time with holes in his sneakers. His father was in the Merchant Marines and later became a factory manager in New York. His mother, Emelina, worked as a nurse in Puerto Rico.

Moving to Puerto Rico at ten was a shock for Jimmy because he had to learn a new language. "I spoke no Spanish," said Jimmy. "But I had to go to school there. It really defined who I am. It formulated my cultural identity."

He often felt like an outsider. To cope with his feelings, he began to pretend—to act. "My childhood has a great deal to do with why I chose [acting]," he said. "You play by yourself a lot. You pretend."

When he was 11, Jimmy and his family moved back to the States from Puerto Rico, settling in Brooklyn, New York. "Trying to fit in with a new group, not having friends, just playing by yourself and making up things—that had a lot to do with planting the seeds of role-playing," Jimmy remembered.

Jimmy attended George Gershwin Junior High, and later, Thomas Jefferson High School in Brooklyn, where he played on the football team. At six feet three inches, he was a natural football player. But he also enjoyed acting

In high school, Jimmy played football and was involved in the drama club.

and got involved in the drama club.
He loved both after-school activities

Jimmy enjoyed acting from the time he was a small boy. Though he participated in several school activities, when there was a conflict, Jimmy chose acting. Today, he is one of the best-known Hispanic actors.

but didn't have time to do them both. He dropped football and stayed with acting.

Then Jimmy starred in the school play. The whole football team came to watch. They sat in the front rows. They were a rowdy bunch, and Jimmy worried that they had brought tomatoes to throw at him. Instead, at the end of the performance, the entire audience stood and clapped. The football players yelled, "Yo, Jim!"

The whole football team came to watch Jimmy in the school play.

Chapter 2
Education of an Actor

Jimmy graduated from high school in 1972. He became a father at 19, when his daughter, Taina, was born. Jimmy and Taina's mother were married and they had a son, Joaquin, several years later. Jimmy was divorced after his son was born, but he has always played an active part in his children's lives.

One thing Jimmy was certain he wanted to do was to continue his education. He entered Brooklyn College and majored in education

Jimmy once thought he'd like to be a teacher.

because he wanted to be a teacher. But even though teaching was what he thought he wanted to do and was what his mother wanted him to do, the call to acting was too strong. He switched his major and graduated with a bachelor's degree in drama from Brooklyn College. A few years later he earned his master of fine arts degree in theater from Cornell University. He was the first in his family to get a college education.

Jimmy says that education is "the key to everything."

His parents and Jimmy have always believed that it is important for all children to get the best education they possibly can. In his talks to schoolkids, Jimmy tells them that education is "the key to everything."

When Jimmy told his family that he wanted to be an actor, his mother was upset at first. She had seen lots of actors in New York City who couldn't get work. She wanted Jimmy to have a steady income.

Jimmy first found acting jobs in front of live audiences in plays staged in New York City. He performed in a production of *Hamlet* directed by Joseph Papp. He was also in the off-Broadway plays *Ballad of Soapy Smith, Buck,* and *Little Victories.*

Jimmy with long-time girlfriend, Wanda De Jesus.

Jimmy continues to love live theater. In 1993, he appeared in a production of *Death and the Maiden* with his long-time girlfriend, Wanda De Jesus.

In his early career and in college, he

studied and performed classic plays—famous dramas that were written long ago and have been performed by generations of actors. Jimmy believes that this kind of education is important for actors. He says that if actors can master these hard roles, they ought to be able to make any character come to life.

Throughout his life, Jimmy has kept his eyes open to things that will make him a better actor. He is always looking to learn new things. He always wants to improve. Once, in college, he even tried ballet to learn about what dancers do.

Jimmy looks for ways to make himself a better actor.

Chapter 3
Television Stardom

Jimmy travels between the East and West Coasts.

Like many busy actors, Jimmy flies back and forth between New York and California. He needs to be near both Hollywood and Broadway. He also wants to see his children, who live in New York. In 1997 his agent was based in California, but his main job, the television show *NYPD Blue*, was filmed in New York.

Jimmy first tested out the acting jobs in California in the mid-eighties, when he landed his first role on a television series. It was a daytime drama, or soap opera, called *All My Children.* Because of his good looks, he has often been cast as a romantic lead. He also appeared on the soap operas *Another World, The Guiding Light,* and *One Life to Live.*

Besides appearing as a love interest, he has also played non-romantic roles, such as criminals, generals, and comic heroes. After being seen by television executives in the daytime dramas, he was cast in nighttime series. His first appearance on prime-time TV was in 1984 when he appeared with Don Johnson in *Miami Vice* as a detective. Unfortunately, his character was killed fifteen minutes into the show! He also appeared on the detective series *Spenser: For Hire.*

His first appearance on prime-time TV was in 1984.

For many years, Jimmy had to take less-than-desirable roles.

For many years, Jimmy had to take less-than-desirable roles. It was several years before he was offered good parts. Finally, he was offered his career-making role. He played Victor Sifuentes, a lawyer, on the hit series *L.A. Law* for six seasons.

Playing Victor Sifuentes put a national spotlight on Jimmy. The part made him a recognized star. It also made history. The role gave Jimmy a chance to play a Hispanic man on a career track—not as a gardener, a peasant, or a drug dealer. It was also a chance to play a good man in a world of shady characters. He told a reporter why the part was so important to him: "I saw this as a chance to establish an intelligent, alternative image [of Hispanics]." Jimmy was aware that many of the roles for Hispanics were as bad people or stereotypes.

He wanted to show TV viewers that Hispanics can be successful,

In 1987, L.A. Law was named Favorite New Dramatic Program at the People's Choice Awards. Here, Jimmy is shown with (left to right) Michael Tucker, Harry Hamlin, Alan Rachins, and Corbin Bernsen.

educated people. In 1988, the Hispanic Bar of Mexico honored him for improving the image of Hispanic lawyers through *L.A. Law*. In 1990, he won television's highest honor, the Emmy Award. He was voted best actor in a dramatic series for *L.A. Law*.

In NYPD Blue, *Jimmy stars with Justine Miceli and Kim Delaney.*

After *L.A. Law* was canceled, Jimmy moved on to other types of television roles. He played in the 1994 made-for-TV movie *The Cisco Kid.* The main character, the Cisco Kid, was a Mexican adventurer and hero who was similar to Robin Hood. Jimmy also played King Solomon in the TV movie *Solomon and Sheba* in 1995. He starred in *Glitz* in 1988 and *The Tommyknockers* in 1993.

His hottest role so far is as Detective Bobby Simone on NBC's police show *NYPD Blue.* He joined the show in 1994 when star David Caruso left after a salary dispute. When Jimmy started on the show, it rose from 29th to 8th in the Nielsen ratings. In this role, Jimmy also plays a strong, smart, caring Latino.

One of his most popular roles so far has been in *NYPD Blue.*

Chapter 4
The Silver Screen

Jimmy's roles in movies have improved since his first one.

Jimmy's roles in movies have improved since his first one. He was first cast as a drug lord in *Running Scared*, a 1986 comedy with Billy Crystal. After that, he starred as a detective in *The Believers* (1987), then played a hero of the Mexican Revolution in *Old Gringo* (1989). He also starred as the romantic leading man in *Fires Within* (1991) and *Switch* (1991).

Old Gringo was based on the book by Mexican writer Carlos

Fuentes. It told the story of a young revolutionary Mexican general

In the movie Old Gringo, *Jimmy played Pancho Villa, a young revolutionary Mexican general.*

named Pancho Villa, who was played by Jimmy. This film gave a much more realistic view of Mexican history than most Hollywood films have portrayed in the past.

Jimmy believes that it's important to show Hispanics in a positive light. But he also says that actors shouldn't limit themselves to

In 1991, Jimmy appeared in the movie, Switch.

one kind of role. "I think that what's important here is to reeducate the powers that be, and the public, that a Hispanic isn't necessarily one type of character or another. It's the same way as an actor's main job is to be versatile. I think he can be both versatile and Hispanic at the same time."

In the Hispanic epic *My Family/ Mi Familia* (1995), Jimmy played a troubled ex-convict trying to figure out what to do with his life. It is perhaps his strongest movie performance to date. The film was written and directed by Gregory Nava. It is the story of several generations of a Mexican American family in Los Angeles. One critic described the way Jimmy performed his role of Jimmy Sanchez as "a terrific and dominant

Jimmy believes it is important to show Hispanics in a positive light.

performance." Jimmy Sanchez is a very bitter person who has served time in prison for killing a man who

In My Family, *Jimmy played ex-convict Jimmy Sanchez.*

killed his wife. An angry widower, he is tricked by his sister into marrying a frightened illegal immigrant. Along the way, Jimmy comes out of his hard, bruised shell and begins to enjoy life again.

Jimmy attended a special screening of *My Family* in Washington, D.C., and was invited to visit President Bill Clinton afterward. *My Family* had one of the most successful limited releases of 1995 and was nominated for an Oscar Award. Jimmy was nominated for an Independent Spirit Award for his performance.

Director Gregory Nava praises Jimmy's work as an actor. "I can't say enough about how talented this man is and what a beautiful person he is to work with," he said. "He's a team player, and he gives all."

Jimmy was nominated for an Oscar for his performance in *My Family*.

Chapter 5
Latino Role Model

Jimmy Smits has probably done more to give national exposure to Hispanics than any other actor. When he saw a problem with the way Hispanics were shown, he spoke up about it and focused his own career on good roles. In this way he is a role model to budding Latino actors.

He also gives back to his community. As a young boy in Brooklyn, he learned that he could

Jimmy is a role model to up-and-coming Latino actors.

Jimmy with Jennifer Lopez (who starred in Selena) *at the National Council of La Raza Awards*

put himself in someone else's shoes. As a seasoned actor, he knows how important the image of himself and his culture can be.

In 1991, citizens of his hometown named him "King of Brooklyn," a title given to ex-Brooklynites who inspire and help their former neighbors.

In 1996 Jimmy hosted a series of television programs called *Hispanic Americans: The New Frontier*. Each show was about the achievements of Latinos. Jimmy hosted these shows to make sure that viewers see Hispanics as they truly are—not as stereotypes. Jimmy explained why this was important to him: "Whether it is film, print, radio, or television, we all have a bond with the media—it shapes and creates the perception and judgments we have of ourselves. . . . It entertains us and

In 1991, he was named "King of Brooklyn."

challenges us, and it takes us to places and events that are normally beyond our reach. It is the window to the world that we access daily. Many people think there is a void in the way Hispanics are being represented."

In 1996 Jimmy won the Hispanic Heritage Award, given to those Hispanics in the public eye who help their communities. He got involved with a task force in 1997 to persuade Hollywood to give Latinos better roles and more chances at office and production jobs in the entertainment industry.

Sometimes, Jimmy finds it difficult to be famous. He doesn't have much privacy. People recognize him everywhere he goes. Being a big star can be stressful. "I don't want people going through

In 1996, Jimmy won the Hispanic Heritage Award.

The 1996 Hispanic Heritage Award recipients attended a news conference in Washington. From left to right: Carmen Votaw, Jimmy Smits, Federico Peña, Isabel Allende, and Oscar de la Renta.

my closet looking at how many pairs of sneakers I have," he said.

He doesn't mind lending his name to worthy causes and serving as a role model for Hispanics. But when it comes to his acting, he says, "Let the work speak for itself." Acting has served him well. And he has done his job with dignity.

Chronology

- Born July 9, 1955, in Brooklyn, New York; mother: Emelina, from Puerto Rico; father: from Suriname, South America
- Attended elementary school in Brooklyn, George Gershwin Junior High, and Thomas Jefferson High School in Brooklyn, graduating in 1972
- Earned B.A. degree in drama from Brooklyn College
- Earned M.A. degree in theater in 1982 from Cornell University
- Got his first television acting job in the daytime drama *All My Children*
- Made his film debut in *Running Scared* in 1986
- Cast as Victor Sifuentes in TV drama *L.A. Law* from 1986 to 1991
- Won an Emmy Award for best actor in a dramatic series (*L.A. Law*) in 1990
- Appeared in several major films, including *Old Gringo, Switch,* and *My Family/Mi Familia*
- In 1991 earned tribute "King of Brooklyn," a title bestowed on ex-Brooklynites who come back to inspire and help their former neighbors
- Received an Emmy, and in 1995 received a Golden Globe Award, for his portrayal of Detective Bobby Simone on *NYPD Blue*
- Won the Hispanic Heritage Award in 1996
- 1997, formed task force to get better jobs for Latinos in Hollywood

Index